## TABLE OF CONTENTS

DISCLAIMER AND TERMS OF USE AGREEMENT:

Introduction

Chapter 1 – Truisms About Advertising

Chapter 2 – Advertising Sucks

Chapter 3 – There are too many ads

Chapter 4 – Truth in Advertising

Chapter 5 – Advertising Discounts: Coupons are often ignored

Chapter 6 – What's Behind Door #1?

I Have a Special Gift for My Readers

Meet the Author

21<sup>st</sup> **Century Marketing Genius**
It's All About the Amount of Ad Impressions You Place
in the Marketplace!!
©Copyright 2013 by Dr. Leland Benton

## DISCLAIMER AND TERMS OF USE AGREEMENT:

**(Please Read This Before Using This Book)**

This information is for educational and informational purposes only. The content is not intended to be a substitute for any professional advice, diagnosis, or treatment.

The authors and publisher of this book and the accompanying materials have used their best efforts in preparing this book.

The authors and publisher make no representation or warranties with respect to the accuracy, applicability, fitness, or completeness of the contents of this book. The information contained in this book is strictly for educational purposes. Therefore, if you wish to apply ideas contained in this book, you are taking full responsibility for your actions.

The authors and publisher disclaim any warranties (express or implied), merchantability, or fitness for any particular purpose. The author and publisher shall in no event be held liable to any party for any direct, indirect, punitive, special, incidental or other consequential damages arising directly or indirectly from any use of this material, which is provided "as is", and without warranties. As always, the advice of a competent legal, tax, accounting, medical or other professional should be sought where applicable.

The authors and publisher do not warrant the performance, effectiveness or applicability of any sites listed or linked to in this book. All links are for information purposes only and are not warranted for content, accuracy or any other implied or explicit purpose. No part of this may be copied, or changed in any format, or used in any way other than what is outlined within this course under any circumstances. Violators will be prosecuted.

This book is © Copyrighted by ePubWealth.com.

## Introduction

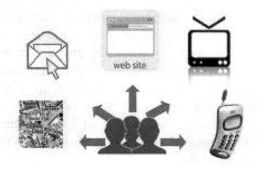

I am often asked what is a 21$^{st}$ Century Marketing Genius and the best answer I can give is a marketing executive that understands the market and consumers he/she is marketing to and is able to pick the appropriate ad medium and ad copy for a successful marketing campaign.

There are literally thousands of ad mediums to choose from and within each medium there are even thousands of more vehicles that deliver ad impressions to consumers but picking the right one...ah, that requires genius!

There is one ad medium and <u>only one</u> that the 21$^{st}$ Century Marketing Genius always falls back on because it is proven and tested and works. Do you know what it is?

Well, stay tuned because we will reveal it to you soon but first let us show you why the 21$^{st}$ Century Marketing Genius always falls back on this one proven medium.

It has been said that "the heart is a lonely hunter" and so is an advertiser that hunts for customers.

But it has also been said that "hunting is for fools who have never heard about bait!"

The 21$^{st}$ Century Marketing Genius does not HUNT for customers; he/she BAITS them! I am not talking about "bait and switch" here. Don't even go there!

I am speaking about baiting the customer with a good story, great selection, great prices, a personal and interactive shopping experience and fantastic service.

**It's all about bait!**

In today's economic landscape, consumers still need to consume and although they are more judicious in their purchases, they will buy from vendors that meet their needs and from vendors that they trust.

But trust is not something that is a given; it has to be earned by an advertiser by consistently providing each consumer with what they need and doing it in a manner that makes it personal and interactive.

There are two main reasons to advertise with the first one being quite obvious:

1. To sell something
2. Branding

Branding is where the consumers recognize your stuff and place a trust factor on it subconsciously.

This can be a good impression or a bad one so positive branding is important!

An apparel site for example, with nothing over $20 has literally over thousands of items in its inventory.

Consumers will always shop for apparel and they will flock to a site like this because the price points are something anyone can afford.

Another brandable item is innovation. The example given above also provides a virtual dressing room where a shopper can uploads his/her body measurements and a head shot photo and then virtually try on any item including cosmetics.

Now that's INNOVATION!

Now ask yourself: why WOULDN'T a shopper buy from this site? The answer is quite obvious – they would and do buy from this site because there is no downside - and the lessons this site provides should be taken seriously when advertising your own stuff.

Next, the ad medium chosen to convey an advertiser's message is as important as the message itself. Many naïve advertisers choose ad mediums based on price alone. This is bad!

Ad mediums must be targeted to the consumers you are going after and only after you have defined your consumer's demographics to a tee.

Target marketing is quickly becoming an art form. Many advertisers can tell you who their customers are exactly but fail to use a targeted ad medium to match its customer's demographics.

So let's discuss this more in detail and then I will reveal the one marketing system that advertisers constantly return to and more so now in today's economic climate.

I will also tell you why they keep returning to this important ad medium and offer you some examples to prove my point.

In numerous surveys conducted (marketing surveys are conducted daily and are too numerous to list) advertising is on the decline insofar as the return on investment. Actual ad placements are not on decline but they are drawing fewer and fewer responses.

Go here for some of the more eye-opening articles:

http://www.reuters.com/article/2012/06/07/us-newspaper-digital-ads-idUSBRE85605E20120607

http://stateofthemedia.org/2012/newspapers-building-digital-revenues-proves-painfully-slow/newspapers-by-the-numbers/

http://paidcontent.org/2012/01/25/419-yahoo-in-context-its-declining-while-the-online-ad-market-keeps-growing/

http://www.mobify.com/blog/declines-in-online-ad-revenues-partly-due-to-ignoring-mobile-visitors/

What is the cause or causes of this phenomenon?

Why are consumers fed up with advertising?

We are going to discuss this in detail taking each truism separately.

It is important to note that although each individual consumer has their own pet peeves when it comes to advertising, the majority find each truism listed here as a center point of focus.

Current trends are demonstrating that consumers are quite literally ignoring or filtering out various forms of advertising.

In short, they actually do not see them and have trained themselves to virtually ignore certain types of ads.

The majority of the ads being ignored are "hype" ads that so obviously attempt to hard sell a consumer.

The second most ignored ads are the really silly ones that attempt to be humorous but in the end are simply ridiculous.

The third category of ads that are most ignored are the ones that are constantly being displayed or shown.

I watched a movie on cable the other evening and the same ad came up on each commercial break. This is not only annoying but just plain silly.

My subconscious mind did such a great job of filtering it out that I am hard pressed to remember what the ad was all about although it was shown over a dozen times during the movie.

The fourth category of ignored ads goes to the ones that are offensive. I personally do not view myself as a prude but I really am not interested in Trojan prophylactics and feminine douche while watching TV.

Like I said, we will get to the truisms one by one but there is a significant lesson that the 21st Century Marketer knows and has learned quite well – BAIT THE CUSTOMER!!!

Now it is important to understand what type of advertiser you are or are assisting in developing ad campaigns for.

live **sustainable**
have **purpose**
seek **change**
savor **fresh**
think **simple**
give **authentic**

1. **Massive & Often** – are advertisers that offer a product/service that consumers DO NOT use every day. These include attorneys, real estate agents/companies, jewelers, appliance stores, etc and because of this fact, these types of advertisers need to advertise massive and often. However; with this said, cost usually prohibits these types of advertisers from advertising massive and often so here is the first reason this type of advertiser returns to use the one and only one ad medium I will reveal in just a minute.

more often

abcdefghijKlm
opqrstuvwxyz
0123456789

2. **Often Only** – are advertisers that have goods and services people use every day like food services, restaurants, dry cleaners, etc. They must advertise often keeping their branding presence in front of consumers but not massively. Statistics show that a storefront business gets most of their customers within a 5-mile radius of the storefront but if branding is done properly, consumers will come from all directions to shop where they feel their needs are met.

3. **Massive only** – are advertisers that offer goods and services that consumers use often but not daily such as auto parts, tires, lube and oil, book stores, car washes, barber and hair salons, massage, etc. These types of businesses must advertise massively but no often...usually about twice a month.

There are exceptions to the list above but most of the exceptions center around the size of the community and the amount of competition.

Most ad mediums ARE NOT designed for massive and often type advertising. The cost is simply prohibited.

Another lesson to learn is what I call combination advertising. By combining more than one ad medium, an advertiser can saturate an area more effectively.

I will speak about this at the end of this book...

## Chapter 2 – Advertising Sucks

Okay, pardon my phraseology but it is true...advertising does suck and it sucks because it more often than not is labeled intrusive by the consumer.

Everyone on the planet has been there; you are watching a great movie and just when it all comes together it breaks for a commercial. That sucks and even if it didn't consumers think it sucks and in advertising, reality means nothing...perception is everything...write that down.

Advertising that doesn't suck tells a story. It can be serious or funny but if it tells a story the consumer will listen. I, personally never miss any of the eTrade commercials with the baby talking or interacting with another baby as grownups. It's funny and I remember the company and what they do because people always remember funny.

Ads/commercials that don't tell a story and are monotonous and repetitious are ignored. If I only had a dime for all of the times I have seen Flo and Progressive

14

Insurance or that little green gecko on Geico commercials, I wouldn't have to write books for a living.

Come on…okay we get it…enough already…sheesh! At least the little green gecko dude is doing some funny stuff lately but Flo has to go!

And while we are bashing auto insurance commercials, 21st Century Auto Insurance sucks too and so does Allstate. They all suck!

But auto insurance doesn't have the market cornered on suck! If I hear that Stanley Steemer Rug Cleaners jingle one more time, I swear I will go out and knife someone.

Or how about those Mesothelioma commercials that attorneys run?

Or my very favorite "Tips from Smokers" with this ugly lady talking through her throat insert.

STOP…PLEASE…just stop…we get it! We may not stop smoking or buy your stuff but we get it.

Remember this: ads/commercials that tell a story sell the most and brand the best.

Where I live a local car dealership runs a commercial of a son graduating from college. His parents buy him a truck and as the dad hands over the keys he says, "In your mind son, you think you have made it. You graduated from college and now have a new truck."

The son is smiling and nodding. The dad continues, "I'm here to tell you that you haven't made it. Every time you achieve something, every time you reach a goal, you are going to think like you made it. I will tell you when you made it!"

The son looks dejected as the commercial segues to his wedding many years later. With a new truck now in the background, the son stands before his dad as his dad says, "Now you have made it, son. Fame and fortune you can lose but the love of a woman is forever.

As the dad walks away he turns and says, "By the way, son, nice truck! Good decision"

Now that is a commercial that sells trucks!

I went down to the dealership to inquire just how successful this commercial is and was astounded to learn that because of this one commercial, this dealership is the number one dealership in the country for this particular brand of truck.

Why? Because it tells a story!

A consumer doesn't mind this type of commercial because they can place themselves within the story. It is all about perception!

Think about it a moment. What ads/commercials catch your attention?

Usually they are funny ones, drama ones like the son and truck one above or most likely ones that have pets and animals in it.

"If we have to do another one of those damn
Coca Cola commercials today, I'm gonna puke ..."

Consumers know what they like so give it to them.

Why produce the same old drivel and drool type of ads/commercials?      Change    up...be    unique    and challenging.

Experiment with different formats and let the consumer decide which is best.

Stay away from ads that suck.  They will be ignored and even provide negative branding.

I don't care if Stanley Steemer is the last carpet cleaner on earth...I WOULD NOT USE THEM BECAUSE I AM SICK OF THAT JINGLE.

How many ads/commercials are you ignoring?   How many does your subconscious mind block out?

I suggest you make a list and you will quickly see just how many ads/commercials you are sick of and purposely block out of your mind.

And you will be amazed that these very same ads/commercials offer products you do not use and would not buy.

## Chapter 3 – There are too many ads

Without a doubt, there are simply too many ads. Numerically speaking, the amount of ads is pushing out the very same content that is drawing the consumer.

I will give you an example. In Las Vegas, every time I visited the place I would listen to this one AM radio station. I liked the music and the fact that it had few commercials.

The last time I was in Las Vegas, there were more commercials than music and I learned the radio station had been sold. I quit listening to it.

It is bad enough when one particular commercial is run over and over again on the same channel or station but it is quite another when there are more commercials than content. Get real!

In newspaper advertising it used to be a 50% ad ratio to content. Today it is over 70% and quickly approaching 80% ad to content ratio.

In 1970, magazine ad to content ration was 46% ads to 54% content. Today it is 54.8% ads to 45.2% content.

Ads are increasing because costs are increasing. Newspapers like the New York Times and Washington Post are hinting that they will begin charging for content.

TV Stations are cutting back in their news departments because of cost.

Radio stations – especially talk radio – are increasing the amount of ads in a given programming session.

I used to listen to talk radio all of the time and enjoyed it until the number of ads became greater than the talk.

But talk radio hosts like the popular Mike Savage, Rush Limbaugh, etc command very high salaries and these high salaries must be made up by increased ad revenue.

In other words, it is not the advertiser's fault; it is the ad medium's fault but the advertiser takes the brunt of consumer frustration.

A recent study looked at sexual *ads* appearing in print and noticed that sexually relevant information sells so *ads* with sexual *content* get noticed. This trend has *increased over* the years: 15 percent of *ads* used sex to sell in 1983 compared to 23% today. WOW! Specifically, alcohol, entertainment and beauty ads are responsible for much of the increase."

Sex sells, or at least that is what advertisers hope. A recent study from the University of Georgia looked at sexual ads appearing in magazines over 30 years and found that the numbers are up.

Sex sells because it attracts attention. People are hard wired to notice anything sensual so ads with sexual content get noticed."

People also are naive to the 'buy this, get this' imagery used in many different types of ads. Some young men actually think Axe body spray will drive women crazy. AMAZING!

One can easily argue that Calvin Klein and Victoria's Secret are not much different than Hanes or Vassarette, but perception studies show those brands are perceived as 'sexy' and some customers want that.

In a study that looked at 3,232 full-page ads published in 1983, 1993 and 2003 in popular magazines Cosmopolitan, Redbook, Esquire, Playboy, Newsweek and Time, researchers found sexual imagery in 20 percent of the ads.

The study also showed sex is primarily used to sell low-risk products purchased on impulse.

Sex is not as effective when selling high-risk, informational products such as banking services, appliances and utility trucks.

The product categories most often found using sexual imagery in advertising were health and hygiene at 38 percent; beauty, 36 percent; drugs and medicine, 29 percent, clothing, 27 percent; travel, 23 percent; and entertainment, 21 percent.

Women are used to sell products most often when pitching sex. In ads sampled from 2003, 92 percent of beauty ads that contained models were female.

With the exception of entertainment advertising, females overwhelming occupy the pages of sex-selling advertisements. Of the 38 percent of provocative health and hygiene advertisements that feature models, 31 percent feature females and 7 percent feature males.

There is one trend advertiser cannot argue; it takes more explicitness to grab our attention and arouse us than before.

## Chapter 4 – Truth in Advertising

It has gotten so bad that most consumers flat out never believe any claim made by advertisers.

The Federal Trade Commission (FTC) is the main federal agency that enforces advertising laws and regulations. Under the Federal Trade Commission Act:

- Advertising must be truthful and non-deceptive
- Advertisers must have evidence to back up their claims
- Advertisements cannot be unfair

Additional laws apply to ads for specialized products like consumer leases, credit, 900 telephone numbers, and products sold through mail order or telephone sales.

State and local governments also regulate advertising, and enforcement is usually the responsibility of a state attorney general, a consumer protection agency or a local district attorney.

With that said above, consumers still don't believe advertising and expect it to mislead and lie.

So let me give you a little background. When man first came upon the earth, his mind was skeptical. When he saw T-Rex eating his friend he knew he had to stay away from that big dude.

As man progressed and became civilized (I say this with tongue in cheek) his mind became gullible. Today people are extremely gullible.

No, Axe Deodorant does not drive women wild.

Porsche cars do not get you the best looking girl. At least the ones you want to take home to mama.

And buying cable instead of Dish will not make you sell your hair to a wig shop.

Get real for goodness sakes!

Yes, these are blatant fabrications but you would be surprised at just how many people fall for this stuff.

Yes, you can even buy very expensive underwear but Fruit of the Loom does the same thing and you can't be more humble than wearing Fruit of the Loom underwear.

That ought to be a bumpersticker.

The blatant stuff aside, the trend to disbelieving anything an advertisement states is increasing.

Here is an editorial from the New York Times dating back to 2009. It pretty much sums up what is going on in the truth area of advertising.

*New York Times Editorial*
*Truth in Advertising, Offline or Online*
*Published: October 12, 2009*

*With so many advertising dollars flowing onto blogs, Facebook and Twitter, it is not surprising that the Federal Trade Commission, which is charged with protecting consumers from sneaky advertising, has turned its eye on this new medium.*

*Spending on consumer-generated and social-networking sites reached $1.01 billion in 2008, up 25 percent from 2007, according to PQ Media, a research firm. It is* *expected to grow about 20 percent this year. Much of this advertising is clearly labeled.*

*But a lot of it is paid advertising masquerading as bona fide endorsements by celebrities, well-known bloggers and even ordinary people — honest comment, free from pecuniary considerations.*

*Companies have been known to make up fake people to blog about their products, such as the two "boys" concocted by Sony to pine over its PSP gaming unit in 2006.*

*Earlier this year, a representative from Belkin offered to pay people to write positive online reviews of its products. There are commercial services to put marketers in contact with bloggers who will tout products for a fee.*

*Deceiving consumers has long been illegal. Guidelines demanding that people who endorse a product for money disclose their connections with advertisers date back to 1980 — way before the age of tweets.*

*In 1968, an F.T.C. advisory demanded that advertorials disclose that they were advertising, not editorial.*

*Concerned over the potential growth of deceptive advertising online, the F.T.C. amended these guidelines recently to clarify that they also apply on blogs, Twitter and other forms of online communication.*

*The rules offline should clearly apply online. This is a matter of principle, not medium, and the new rules are not an excessive burden.*

*The guidelines state that endorsers must disclose payments in cash or in kind from companies whose products they endorse. Telling a commentator flogging a product online to disclose commercial ties does not constitute a challenge to free speech.*

*Still, regulators should tread carefully. As it enforces rules about disclosure of product endorsements on the Internet's platforms, the F.T.C. must care not to hamstring the ability of bloggers and Twitterers to report and comment about the world.*

*To stay on the safe side, regulators should focus enforcement on the advertising companies rather than on the bloggers.*

*Advertisers are the drivers of this new trend. The onus should be on them to ensure that blogs pitching their stuff warn readers about the commercial motivation of the endorsements.*

*But disclosure is a reasonable demand to make in any medium. It protects consumers and bolsters the bonds of trust between writers and their audience.*

Is it safe to assume that the FTC has everything under control?

No way, Jose!

They can barely keep up with just the big stuff and deceptions/frauds.

"Buyer Beware" must always be a consumer's credo. Shame on you, if you allow government to protect you!

**This is truthful!**

**But is this?**

## Chapter 5 – Advertising Discounts: Coupons are often ignored

Coupons used to be the rage but a good many consumers hated cutting them out and redeeming them at the vendor.

Then digital coupons came out and a consumer could even redeem them right off their cell phone.

Now, diminishing returns has set in where the consumer not only demands and expects coupons, but the coupons themselves have to have intrinsic value for the consumer to even consider them.

Gone are the days of 10% off and 20% off.

Consumers now want 2-for-1 and the perception that a coupon is offering a true "deal"!

Here is a transcript of a couponer interacting with a cashier…

*I had a similar experience in FL yesterday. Went through the checkout and handed over my q's. Had a q for a free Thomas' item that I received in the mail. It was obviously from the company (foil backing, hologram...) Anyway, the cashier needed an over-ride and called for the mgr who actually SMELLED the q and asked me if I made it! I was shocked! Told her the company had mailed it to me and pointed out the security features on it. She ended up taking it, but as I left, I heard her commenting to the cashier that it was obviously a fraud. I should have gone back and confronted her, but thought it best to hold my tongue and calm down. (Also felt bad for the line of customers behind me having to wait through all of this)*

This is not a rare occurrence because coupon fraud is rampant. But as I have stated a couple of times previously, perception is everything or in other words perception is reality. To add fuel to the argument above read the following blog post.

*Perception is Reality. Does That Make Groupon a Gift Card?*

*Posted on January 26, 2011 by --Jeff Yablon/The Answer Guy-- Business Change & SEO Consultant*

*Is Groupon in the Gift Card Business? Do they sell Coupons? Maybe Groupon is trafficking in Gift Cards.*

*Do you care which discount-providing item Groupon sells? To my dismay, some people are starting to debate the idea, apparently with the goal of compelling Groupon to make the amazing deals they offers never expire.*

*Talk about Perception Being Reality (and I have, several times; my most recent "Perception is Reality" post is here)!*

*If you've somehow missed it, even among the recent news that they had turned down an offer to be acquired by Google for $6 Billion, Groupon is a website offering some pretty amazing deals each day.*

*The discounts are huge, the deals expire, and so does your window to use the deals, which you pay for before you use them. It's "like" buying a gift card.*

*Problem is, there are laws that govern gift card expiration. So if Groupon is selling those, then in many places they can't expire.*

*Are They?*

*Perception is Reality, and I'm not an attorney. Let's approach this from a pure customer service perspective.*

*Groupon, of course would claim that they aren't selling "gift cards" at all, if only to avoid the legal issues.*

*They might believe they're selling coupons, which can expire.*

*They might even believe they've come up with an entirely new category of customer service/discounting vehicle.*

*But ask yourself a question: should it matter?*

*Like millions of people, I regularly receive coupons in the mail from Bed Bath and Beyond. The coupons have clear expiration dates printed on them.*

*And while I don't believe this to be their official policy, Bed Bath and Beyond honors coupons even if they've expired.*

*They don't have to do that, and I don't think too many people would storm out of their local Bed Bath and Beyond never to return if they were told they were trying to use expired coupons.*

*Bed Bath and Beyond has simply decided to skirt this perception/reality issue (or create a greater perception and reality) by providing superb customer service.*

***Why would you tell a customer that you wanted their business under certain conditions yesterday, but that you think less of their business today?***

*There might be an answer to that, along the lines of "my business is successful enough now that I no longer need to 'buy' business", but that isn't the mechanism behind coupon expiration dates.*

*Coupons expire to create a sense of urgency in buyers; if you already have someone's money, there's no need for an expiration date in that regard.*

*There's also no "accounting" issue. You book the income as soon as you collect the money.*

*So this can be a pure customer service conversation. Groupon and its partners don't have to apply those expiration dates.*

*Groupon customers just need for their perception to include the reality that the businesses from which they buy Groupon deals might not be able to accommodate them easily farther down the road, or might even have gone out of business if the coupons are held for too long a period.*

*But frankly, those realities apply even when you use a Groupon coupon during a stated pre-expiration period.*

*See? Perception is reality. All you need to do to create excellent customer service is . . . everything.*

Here is the part I want you to see…**Why would you tell a customer that you wanted their business under certain conditions yesterday, but that you think less of their business today?**

**This is important because coupons can cause more problems than good. The intent of coupons is to provide a little extra push towards a buying decision.**

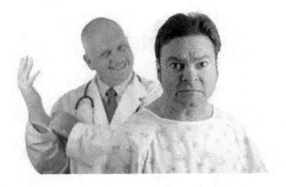

But the perception can easily change if redeeming the coupon brings some unwanted exchanges.

Use coupons that offer true value and have a good perception or do not use them at all.

The main consideration to coupon usage should be in the ease of redemption as much as the offer itself.

I place expiration dates on all of my coupons but ignore them at redemption and honor them even after the expiration date.

## Chapter 6 – What's Behind Door #1?

Now it is time to reveal the one and only marketing system that advertisers of all types and sizes keep returning to time and time again.

I think you are going to be surprised.

Ready?

Yep – email it is! I can remember many gurus predicting the demise of email.

RSS was supposed to be its doom but this never occurred. In fact RSS is in decline rather than email.

But why email?  What makes it so resilient?

Email has been around since 1965.  Yes, but it never became very popular until about 1969.  Throughout the 70s and early 80s, email was only popular with large corporations and universities.

But in 1989, MCIMail came out and email became available to the general public.  From 1989 till 1996, email was the only marketing system on the net.  Other marketing systems were introduced such as pay-per-click, banner advertising, etc but none of them have lasted as long as email.

The reason is because email is inexpensive, far-reaching, quick to employ and with a very small learning curve.

There are many different types of email marketing companies but I will concentrate on the most important on – BOUTIQUE Email Marketing.

Boutique Email Marketers are completely turnkey. They do everything – provide the list, delivery and even provide the HTML email that is delivered.

They operate suing packages that apply to all size businesses. Here is an example of a boutique email marketer:

# EmailNations

http://Emailnations.com

Click on the Sign Up and Pricing tab on the menu bar and checkout their pricing structure.

What is unique about this company is that their packages are for complete counties so you can literally saturate a geographic area for a very small price.

I have used this company to market a good many of my books and because of the return, I have pretty much discontinued all other forms of advertising.

For example, I used EmailNations to send an text email ad for my book "The Power of Observation". I chose Los Angeles County with a little over 6-million names and sold 1688 books in one day.

One huge benefit of email marketing is that the ad impression is not shared by any other offer. I have placed ads in newspapers and I couldn't even find them let alone a consumer. No one shares your ad impression. The consumer only sees what you want them to see.

Second, the metrics provided by each campaign allows you to fine-tune your results and that makes it really nice.

Next, email marketing is highly targeted. In short, there is no downside to email marketing and with a little practice you too can use it most effectively.

I have identified over 200-boutique email house with different offers and that have access to different lists. For a personal copy of this list email me at [mailto:support@epubwealth.com](mailto:support@epubwealth.com) and I will send it right out.

To summarize, email is effective, low-cost, highly targeted, turnkey and comes with great results. Be careful in choosing the email house. Be sure their lists are fresh and optin. And be sure they supply you with the metrics from each campaign.

The 21st Century Marketing Genius knows email rocks and keeps returning on investment long after other ad mediums have failed.

Now it is your turn...

## I Have a Special Gift for My Readers

I appreciate my readers for without them I am just another author attempting to make a difference. If my book has made a favorable impression please leave me an honest review.    Thank you in advance for you participation.

My readers and I have in common a passion for the written word as well as the desire to learn and grow from books.

My special offer to you is a massive ebook library that I have compiled over the years. It contains hundreds of fiction and non-fiction ebooks in Adobe Acrobat PDF format as well as the Greek classics and old literary classics too.

In fact, this library is so massive to completely download the entire library will require over 5 GBs open on your desktop.

Use the link below and scan all of the ebooks in the library. You can select the ebooks you want individually or download the entire library.

The link below does not expire after a given time period so you are free to return for more books rather than clog your desktop. And feel free to give the link to your friends who enjoy reading too.

I thank you for reading my book and hope if you are pleased that you will leave me an honest review so that I can improve my work and or write books that appeal to your interests.

Okay, here is the link…

http://tinyurl.com/special-readers-promo

PS: If you wish to reach me personally for any reason you may simply write to mailto:support@epubwealth.com.

I answer all of my emails so rest assured I will respond.

## Meet the Author

Dr. Leland Benton is Director of Applied Web Info, a holding company for ePubWealth.com, a leading ePublisher company based in Utah. With over 21,000 resellers in over 22-countries, ePubWealth.com is a leader in ePublishing, book promotion, and ebook marketing.

As the creator and author of "The ePubWealth Program," Leland teaches up-and-coming authors the ins-and-outs of today's ePublishing world. He has assisted hundreds of authors make it big in the ePublishing world.

Leland also created a series of external book promotion programs and teaches authors how to promote their books using external marketing sources.

Leland is also the Managing Director of Applied Mind Sciences, the company's mind research unit and Chief Forensics Investigator for the company's ForensicsNation unit. He is active in privacy rights through the company's PrivacyNations unit and is an expert in survival planning and disaster relief through the company's SurvivalNations unit.

Leland resides in Southern Utah.

**Visit some of his websites**
http://www.AddMeInNow.com
http://www.AppliedMindSciences.com
http://www.AppliedWebInfo.com

http://www.BookbuilderPLUS.com
http://www.BookJumping.com
http://www.EmailNations.com
http://www.EmbarrassingProblemsFix.com
http://www.ePubWealth.com
http://www.ForensicsNation.com
http://www.ForensicsNationStore.com
http://www.FreebiesNation.com
http://www.HealthFitnessWellnessNation.com
http://www.Neternatives.com
http://www.PrivacyNations.com
http://www.RetireWithoutMoney.org
http://www.SurvivalNations.com
http://www.TheBentonKitchen.com
http://www.Theolegions.org
http://www.VideoBookbuilder.com

**Some Other Books You May Enjoy From
ePubWealth.com, LLC Library Catalog**

**EPW Library Catalog Online**
http://www.epubwealth.com/wp-content/uploads/2013/07/Leland-benton-private-turbo.pdf

**EPW Library Catalog Download**
http://www.filefactory.com/f/562ef3ea1a054f0a

www.ingramcontent.com/pod-product-compliance
Lightning Source LLC
Chambersburg PA
CBHW071034050326
40689CB00014B/3642